W9-BMD-405

Sun, Moon, and Stars

Developed at
Lawrence Hall of Science
University of California at Berkeley

Published and Distributed by **Delta Education**,
a member of the School Specialty Family

1012446
978-1-59821-783-4

Printing 5 — 6/2010
Worldcolor, Leominster, MA

The FOSS program began at the Lawrence Hall of Science as a science enrichment program. Over the past 25 years, with the support of the National Science Foundation and the University of California at Berkeley, the program has evolved into a total curriculum for all students and their teachers, grades K–6. The program reflects significant contributions of dedicated professionals in the classroom, their students, administrators, parents, and members of the scientific community. We acknowledge the thousands of educators who have given life to the ideas embodied in the FOSS program. We acknowledge and thank them all for their contributions to the development and implementation of FOSS.

FOSS © 2009 and © 2007 Lawrence Hall of Science Team

Larry Malone and Linda De Lucchi, FOSS Project Codirectors and Lead Developers; Kathy Long, Assessment Coordinator; Teri Dannenberg, Developer; Susan Kaschner Jagoda, Developer; Ann Moriarty, Developer; Kimi Hosoume, Developer; Deanne Giffin, Early Childhood Consultant; Joanna Totino, EL Consultant and Professional Developer; Jaine Kopp and Jenny Maguire, Mathematics Consultants; David Lippman, Editor and Program Specialist; Carol Sevilla, Publications Design Coordinator; Rose Craig, Illustrator; Susan Stanley and Carol Bevilacqua, Graphic Production; Susan Ketchner, Multimedia Director; Alana Chan, Nicole Alexis Medina, and Kate Jordan, FOSSweb Producers; Roseanna Yau and Leigh Anne McConnaughey, Multimedia Artist and Designer; Dan Bluestein, Programmer; Roger Vang, Programmer; Christopher Cianciarulo, Programmer; John Quick, Photographer

FOSS © 2009 and © 2007 Delta Education Team

Bonnie Piotrowski, FOSS Editorial Director

Project Team: Jennifer Apt, Mathew Bacon, Lynne Bleeker, Tom Guetling, Joann Hoy, Lisa Lachance, Katrina Lewin, Elizabeth Luzadre, Paulette Miley, Sandra Mitchell, Cathrine Monson, Cyndy Patrick, John Prescott, Gary Standafer, Heidi Tyson, Nina Whitney

FOSS © 2009 and © 2007 Content Reviewers

David M. Andrews, EdD, Professor of Biology and Science Education and Executive Director, Science and Mathematics Education Center, California State University, Fresno, CA

Carol Balfe, PhD, Science Education Consultant and Former Research Scientist, Oakland, CA

Ellen P. Metzger, PhD, Professor of Geology, California State University, San Jose, CA

FOSS © 2009 and © 2007 Teacher Reviewers

Amy Edmindson, Centralia School, Anaheim, CA; Amy Hellewell, Bonita Canyon School, Irvine, CA; Bonney Waters, Two Bunch Palms Elementary, Desert Hot Springs, CA; Christina Lambie, Highland Elementary, Richmond, CA; Debby Palmer, Turtle Rock Elementary, Irvine, CA; Heinrich Sartin, District 2 Office, North Hollywood, CA; Jeff Self, Washington Elementary, Eureka, CA; Jennifer Faulhaber, G. H. Dysinger School, Buena Park, CA; Jill Garmon, Brywood Elementary, Irvine, CA; Don McKenney, Oakland Unified School District, Oakland, CA; Jill Miles, Sheridan School, Sheridan, CA; Jim Jones, Valley View School, Coachella, CA; Joy Peoples, Riverside School, Riverside, CA; Katherine Jacobs, Verde School, Irvine, CA; Kathy Albrecht, Heritage Oak School, Roseville, CA; Lauren Vu-Tran, Fountain Valley School, Fountain Valley, CA; Lillian Valadez-Rodela, San Pedro MST, San Pedro, CA; Lori Van-Gorp, Anaheim Hills Elementary, Anaheim, CA; Maura Crossin, Local District 4, Los Angeles, CA; Melissa Tallman, College Park Elementary, Irvine, CA; Nancy Lester, Newport Elementary, Newport Beach, CA; Pamela Rockwell, Anaheim Hills Elementary, Anaheim, CA; Rhonda Lemon, Danbrook School, Anaheim, CA; Sherri Ferguson, Brywood Elementary, Irvine, CA; Susan Liberati, Beverly Hills School District, Beverly Hills, CA; Will Neddersen, Tustin USD, Tustin, CA

Production for © 2007 and © 2003 Editions

LaurelTech Integrated Publishing Services

FOSS © 1993–2003 Edition Staff and Contributors

Professor Lawrence F. Lowery, Principal Investigator; Linda De Lucchi, Codirector; Larry Malone, Codirector; Kathy Long, Assessment Coordinator; Leigh Agler, Developer; Susan Kaschner Jagoda, Developer; Kari Rees, Reading Consultant; Carol Sevilla, Graphic Designer; Rose Craig, Illustrator

Contributors: Sara Armstrong, John Quick, Eileen Massey, Joanna Totino, Denise Soderlund, Laura Loutit, Eric Crane, Yiyu Xie, Marco Molinaro, Susan Ketchner, Joanna Gladden, Lisa Haderlie-Baker, Sandra Ragan, Cheryl Webb, Alev Burton, Mark Warren, Marshall Montgomery

FOSS © 2000–2003 Delta Education Team

Mathew Bacon, Grant Gardner, Tom Guetling, Joann Hoy, Dana Koch, Lisa Lachance, Cathrine Monson, Kerri O'Donnell, Bonnie Piotrowski, John Prescott, Jeanette Wall

FOSS Grades K–6 Revision © 2000–2003 Teacher Associates
Claire Kelley, Dennett Elementary School, Plympton, MA
Dyan Van Bishler, Clyde Hill Elementary, Bellevue, WA
Sig Doran, Clyde Hill Elementary, Bellevue, WA
Ann Kumata, John Muir Elementary, Seattle, WA
Kate Shonk, Pleasant Valley Primary, Vancouver, WA
Theresa Fowler, John Rogers Elementary, Seattle, WA
Andrea Edwards, Woodland Primary School, Woodland, WA
Deanne Giffin and Janet Gay, Bancroft Elementary School, Walnut Creek, CA
Jill Kraus, Hawthorne Elementary School, Oakland, CA
Brenda Redmond, Los Perales School, Moraga, CA
Catherine Behymer, Napa Valley Language Academy, Napa, CA
Alison McSweeney, Dennett Elementary, Plympton, MA
Helen Howard and Carol Strandberg, Mt. Erie Elementary, Anacortes, WA
Rondi Peth, Dawn Mayer, and Jeannette Beatty, Fidalgo Elementary, Anacortes, WA
Virginia Kammer, Fresno Unified School District, Fresno, CA
Henrietta Griffitts and Jackie Meylan Dodge, Mt. Diablo Unified School District, Concord, CA

Production for © 2000 Edition *FOSS Science Stories*
Creative Media Applications, Inc.
Rhea Baehr, Writer; Michael Burgan, Writer; Robin Doak, Writer; Matthew Dylan, Writer; Emily Lauren, Writer; Matt Levine, Editor; Joanne Mattern, Writer; Dona Smith, Writer; Fabia Wargin, Graphic Designer

Original FOSS © 1993–1995 Grades K–6 School District Partners
Kathy Jacobsen, Mt. Diablo Unified School District
Judy Guilkey-Amado and Alexa Hauser, Vallejo City Unified School District
Richard Merrill, Mt. Diablo Unified School District

Original FOSS © 1993–1995 Grades K–6 National Trials Center Directors and Advisers
Directors:
Ramona Anshutz, Kansas State Dept. of Education; Ron Bonnstetter, University of
Nebraska; John Cairns, Delaware Dept. of Public Instruction; Arthur Camins, CSD #16,
Brooklyn, NY; Winston Hoskins, Garland Independent School District, TX; Rhoda Immer,
Siskiyou County Office of Education, CA; Mildred Jones, New York City Schools;
Floyd Mattheis, East Carolina University, NC; Alan McCormack, San Diego State
University; Don McCurdy, University of Nebraska; Joseph Premo, Minneapolis Schools;
John Staver, Kansas State University, Manhattan, KS; Brian Swagerty, Siskiyou County
Office of Education, CA; Sandra Wolford, Colonial School District, New Castle, DE

Advisers:
Sara Armstrong, Heidi Bachman, Carl Berger, Donna Dailey, Robert Dean, Steve Essig, Rosella
Jackson, Marsha Knudsen, Catherine Koshland, Samuel Markowitz, Glenn McGlathery, Margaret
McIntyre, Shirley McKinney, Richard Merrill, Marshall Montgomery, Gary Nakagiri, Karen Ostlund,
John Schippers, Dave Stronck, Dean Taylor, Judy Van Hoorn

FOSS © 1993–1995 Grades K–6 National Trials Leadership Partners
David Allard, Hal Benham, Diane Benham, Arthur Camins, Vicki Clark, John Clementson, Cathy
Klinesteker, Karen Dawkins, Sally Dudley, Sheila Dunston, Steve Essig, Fred Fifer, Theresa
Flaningam, Chris Foster, Robert Grossman, Cynthia Ledbetter, Charlotte McDonald, Karen Ostlund,
Janet Posen, Carlton Robardey, Twyla Sherman, Gerald Skoog, Dean Taylor, Mary Zapata

Published and Distributed by Delta Education, a member of the School Specialty Family

The FOSS program was developed in part with the support of the National Science Foundation grant
nos. MDR-8751727 and MDR-9150097. However, any opinions, findings, conclusions, statements, and
recommendations expressed herein are those of the authors and do not necessarily reflect the views of NSF.

Table of Contents

Sunrise and Sunset

n the picture below the **Sun** is just coming up. It is **sunrise.** What direction are you looking?

Sun rising over Mt. Whitney, Sequoia National Park, California

East. The Sun always rises in the east. If you are in Pittsburgh, Pennsylvania, the Sun rises in the east. If you are in Raleigh, North Carolina, the Sun rises in the east. If you are in Dallas, Texas, the Sun rises in the east. It doesn't matter where you are on Earth. The Sun rises in the east.

In this picture the Sun is just going down. It is **sunset.**
What direction are you looking now?

Sun setting over the Golden Gate Bridge in San Francisco, California

West. The Sun always sets in the west. If you are in Pittsburgh, Pennsylvania, the Sun sets in the west. If you are in Raleigh, North Carolina, the Sun sets in the west. If you are in Dallas, Texas, the Sun sets in the west. It doesn't matter where you are on Earth. The Sun sets in the west.

Every day the Sun rises in the east and sets in the west. To get from east to west, the Sun slowly travels across the sky. In the early morning, when the Sun first comes up, it is touching the **horizon** in the east. At noon the Sun is at its highest position in the sky. At sunset the Sun is touching the horizon in the west. The Sun's position in the sky changes all day long.

What Makes the Sun Move?

The Sun looks like it moves across the sky. But it really doesn't. It is the planet Earth that is moving. Here's how it works.

Earth is spinning like a top. It takes 1 day for Earth to go around once. Because we are turning, half of the time we are on the sunny side of Earth. We call the sunny side **day.** The other half of the time we are on the dark side. We call the dark side **night.**

Earth turns toward the east. So the Sun seems to move from east to west across the sky.

Pretend it's just before sunrise. You can't see the Sun because you are still on the dark side of Earth. But in 5 minutes, Earth turns just enough for you to see the Sun peeking over the horizon. That moment is sunrise.

Earth turns toward the east, the direction of the orange arrow. That means the first sunlight of the day will be in the east. And, of course, Earth keeps turning. You keep moving with it. Four or 5 hours later, you have turned so far that the Sun is high over your head. And 5 hours after that, the Sun is low in the western sky. This is because Earth is moving in an eastward direction. It looks like the Sun is moving across the sky in a westward direction. Now it is sunset. The Sun slips below the horizon in the west. It is dark again.

Review Questions

1. **Where does the Sun rise and where does it set?**

2. **How does the Sun move from sunrise to sunset?**

Changing Shadows

Objects, such as people, buildings, and flagpoles, have **shadows** on sunny days. That's because solid objects block the **sunlight.** Shadows give information about the position of the Sun. What if you see your shadow in front of you? You would know the Sun is behind you.

Did you know a shadow can tell you what time of day it is? Here's how. Pretend you are standing in the picture below. You are facing south. North is behind you. It's 12:00 noon. The Sun is in the south and high overhead.

Look at the shadow of the flagpole in illustration 1. What direction is it pointing? It is pointing straight north. And it is short. When a shadow points north, the time is about 12:00 noon.

What did the shadow look like at 9:00 this morning? Do you remember what direction your shadow pointed in the morning? Do you remember how long it was?

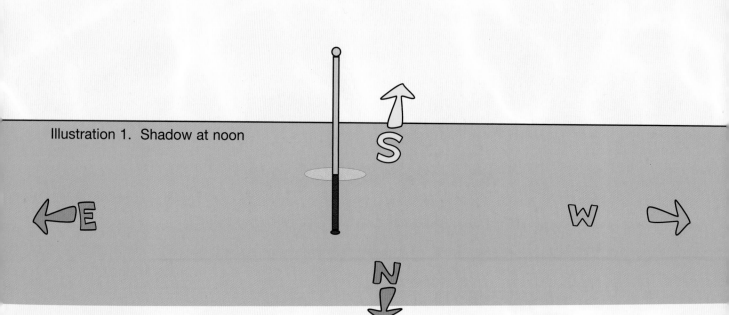

Illustration 1. Shadow at noon

Illustration 2 shows the flagpole at 9:00 in the morning. The flagpole casts a long shadow and the shadow points west. But the shadow doesn't point straight west. It points a little bit north, too. The direction between north and west is called northwest.

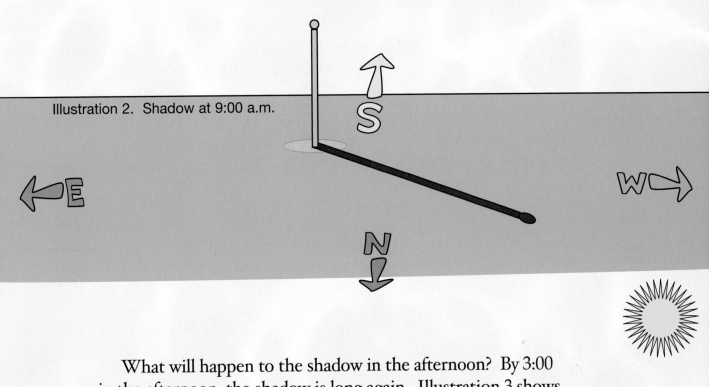

Illustration 2. Shadow at 9:00 a.m.

What will happen to the shadow in the afternoon? By 3:00 in the afternoon, the shadow is long again. Illustration 3 shows the shadow pointing east. Actually, it is pointing northeast. The Sun has moved across the sky and looks low in the west. In a few more hours the Sun will set in the west.

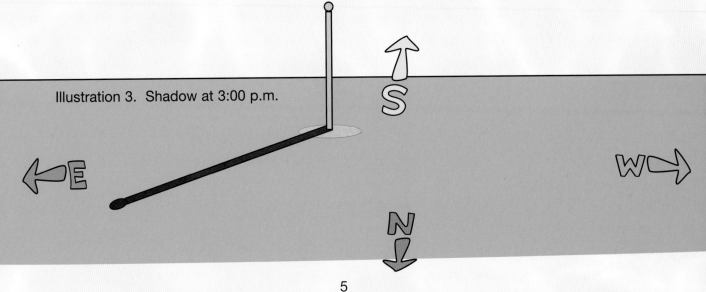

Illustration 3. Shadow at 3:00 p.m.

Two things happen to shadows between sunrise and sunset. Early in the morning, shadows are long and they point west. As time passes, the Sun rises higher in the sky. The Sun is moving from east to west. As the Sun moves, shadows get shorter and shorter. And they point more and more north.

At noon the shadow is as short as it will get. It points straight north. After noon, the Sun keeps moving across the sky. Shadows get longer and point more to the east. Just before sunset, shadows are very long and they point east.

See how shadows can work like a clock? Here is a picture with several shadows and their times. All you need is a pole in the ground and a sunny day.

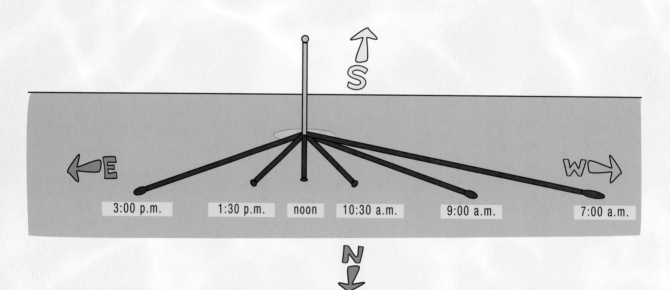

Sun and Seasons

Shadows can tell us even more about the movement of the Sun. We know the Sun moves across the sky from east to west every day. But did you know that the Sun also changes position in the sky from **season** to season? Here's how you can prove it.

Pretend you are looking at the flagpole again. But this time you are standing on the east side of the pole facing west. North is to your right and south is to your left.

For this experiment you have to measure the shadow at noon only. But you have to measure it every day for a year!

Here are the noon shadows for just five times during the year. Look at the length of the shadow and the position of the Sun in the sky on each date.

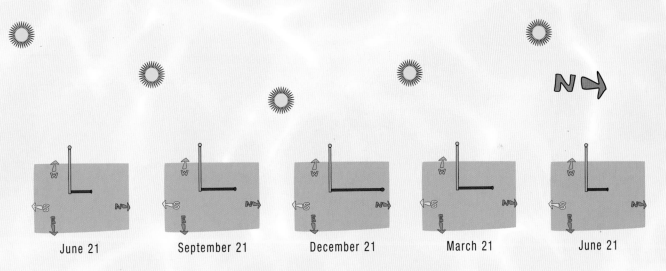

Sun position and shadow length at noon on 5 days during a year

On June 21, the first day of summer, the Sun is high in the sky at noon. Three months later, on September 21, the first day of fall, the Sun is lower. And on December 21, the first day of winter, the Sun is at its lowest noon position. After December 21 the Sun begins to climb higher in the sky again. On March 21 it is as high as it was in September. One year after starting the experiment, on June 21, the Sun is again at its highest noon position.

The Sun's change of position in the sky minute by minute during a day is **predictable.** The Sun's position in the sky season to season during a year is also predictable.

Review Questions

1. **How does the Sun's position in the sky change over a day?**

2. **In what ways do shadows change during a day?**

3. **What causes shadows to change during a day?**

4. **Think about a flagpole. How does its shadow change over a year?**

Summary:
The Sun

There is one thing you can depend on for sure. The **Sun** will come up tomorrow morning. And you can be sure it will come up in the east. At the end of the **day,** it will set in the west. Count on it.

As the day goes along, the Sun travels across the sky from east to west. And it rises higher and higher in the sky. At noon it is at its highest position in the sky. From noon to sunset the Sun continues to travel west. And it gets lower and lower in the sky. At sunset the Sun disappears below the horizon in the west. Another day has passed. And tomorrow will be the same.

Well, almost the same. A careful observer will notice that the Sun's path through the sky is a tiny bit different every day. You can see the difference by studying **shadows.**

9

A shadow is the dark area behind an object. A shadow is created where an object blocks **sunlight.** A steel pole, like a flagpole, will cast a shadow. The direction of the pole's shadow changes as the Sun's position changes. At noon the Sun is highest in the sky. Noon is also when the flagpole's shadow is the shortest of the day.

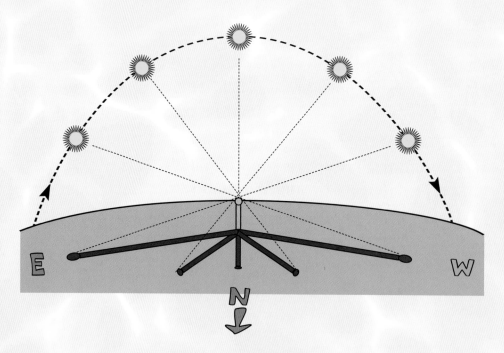

The Sun's position changes all day from sunrise to sunset.

The noon shadow is the one to look at to see how the Sun's position changes **season** to season. The length of that shadow changes a little bit every day. Why does the length of the shadow change? Because the position of the Sun at noon changes a little bit every day.

The pattern of change is **predictable.** The position of the noon Sun gets higher in the sky from December 21 to June 21. On June 21 the Sun is highest in the sky. That's also the day when the flagpole's shadow is the shortest of the year.

The position of the noon Sun gets lower in the sky each day between June 21 and December 21. On December 21 the Sun is lowest in the noon sky. That's also the day that the flagpole's shadow is longest of the year.

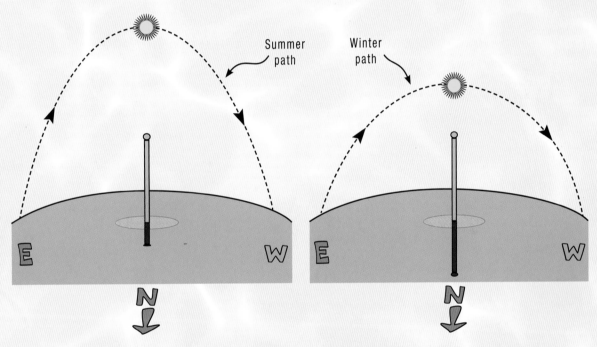

The Sun's path through the sky is higher in the summer.

The Sun's position in the sky changes in two ways. Every day the Sun rises in the east, travels a path across the sky, and sets in the west. The other way the Sun's position changes is where the daily path goes. In the summer the Sun's path is high in the sky. In the winter the Sun's path is low in the sky.

Summary Questions

Now is a good time to review what you have recorded in your science notebook. Think about the connection between the position of the Sun in the sky and the shadows cast by objects in the sunlight.

1. What two ways does the Sun's position in the sky change?

2. What are shadows and what causes them?

3. What causes shadows to change size and direction during a day?

4. Describe the Sun's change of position in the sky during 1 day.

5. Describe the Sun's change of position in the sky during 1 year.

Vocabulary

Sun

day

shadow

sunlight

season

predictable

Extensions

Math Problem of the Week

Bert and Anna were observing shadows on the same day. Bert observed shadows made by a pole 1 meter tall. Anna observed shadows made by a pole 2 meters tall.

Bert's data

Time	Length (cm)
9:00 a.m.	320
12:00 noon	80
2:00 p.m.	240

Anna's data

Time	Length (cm)
10:00 a.m.	480
12:00 noon	160
3:00 p.m.	640

1. How long was Bert's shadow at 10:00 a.m.? How do you know?

2. How long was Anna's shadow at 9:00 a.m.? How do you know?

3. How long was Bert's shadow at 3:00 p.m.? How do you know?

4. At what time was Anna's shadow the same length as Bert's 9:00 a.m. shadow? How do you know?

Home/School Connection

Before mechanical clocks were invented, people used sundials to tell the time. You can make a model sundial at home. Ask your teacher for a sheet with the instructions.

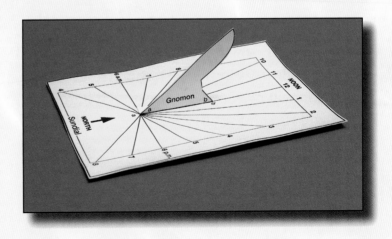

The Night Sky

What do you see when you look up at the sky? During the day you see the Sun. Sometimes you can see the **Moon.** You might see clouds. If you watch long enough, you will see something fly by, such as a bird or an airplane.

At night you can see different things in the sky. When the Moon is up, it is the brightest object in the night sky. The Moon might look like a thin sliver. Or it might be big and round.

You might see the Moon in the west. When the Moon is in the west, it will set soon. The Moon could be in the east. When the Moon is in the east, it is rising. It is easy to predict when the Sun will rise and set. It is much harder to predict when the Moon will rise and set.

Stars

When it is clear, you can see **stars** in the night sky. Night is the only time you can see stars. Well, almost the only time. There is one star we can see in the daytime. It's the Sun. Our star shines so brightly that it is impossible to see the other stars. But after the Sun sets, we can see that the sky is full of stars. It looks like there are millions of stars in the sky on a clear night. But actually you can see only about 2,000 with your **unaided eyes.**

On a clear night, you can see about 2,000 stars in the sky.

Planets

Some stars are brighter than others. They are the first ones you can see just after the Sun sets. Did you ever make a wish on the first star that appears in the evening sky? "Star light, star bright, first star I see tonight. I wish I may, I wish I might, have the wish I make tonight." But the star that you make a wish on may not be a star at all. The brightest stars are actually **planets.**

Earth **orbits** the Sun with seven other planets and several dwarf planets. Five of them can be seen in the night sky. Venus is one of the planets you might see. Ancient sky watchers called Venus the evening star. This was because it was often seen near the western horizon after sunset. Venus was also called the morning star. It was also seen near the eastern horizon just before sunrise. What caused the confusion?

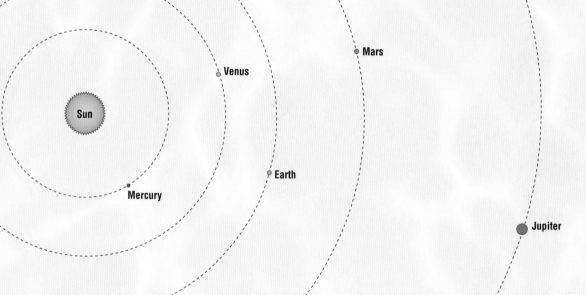

Five planets orbiting the Sun with Earth can be seen in the night sky.

Two planets orbit closer to the Sun than Earth does. Mercury is closest to the Sun. Then comes Venus. Because Venus orbits closer to the Sun, sometimes it shows up just before sunrise as the morning star. A few months later, Venus is on the other side of the Sun. Now it shows up after sunset as the evening star. That's why night-sky observers thought Venus was two different stars.

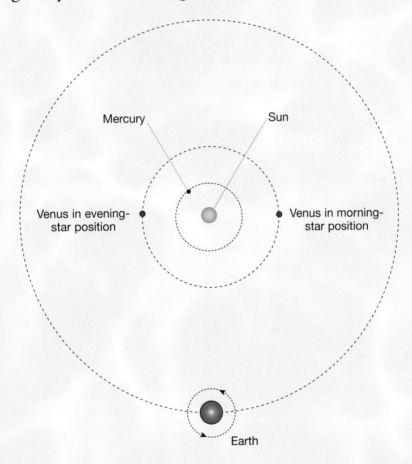

Mercury

Sun

Venus in evening-
star position

Venus in morning-
star position

Earth

Four other planets can be seen with unaided eyes. Mercury is visible sometimes. Because it is so close to the Sun, it is often lost in the bright glare of the Sun. Mars is the fourth planet from the Sun. It shines with a slightly red light. Jupiter and Saturn are the farthest of the visible planets. Still, they are pretty bright because they are so big.

It is a special night when you can see all five planets together in the night sky. It doesn't happen very often. It happened in 2004. It won't happen again until 2036!

Review Questions

1. **What are some of the objects you can see in the night sky that you can't see during the day?**

2. **Which object is the brightest object in the night sky?**

3. **Which star is the closest to planet Earth?**

4. **Look at the picture of the crescent Moon below. What is the other bright object you can see in the night sky?**

An astronomer looking at the night sky just after sunset

Changing Moon

Earth has one large **satellite.** It is called the Moon. The Moon completes one orbit around Earth every 28 days. One complete orbit is also called a **cycle.**

The Moon is the second-brightest object in the sky. It shines so brightly that you can see it even during the day. But did you know that the Moon doesn't make its own light? The light you see coming from the Moon is **reflected** sunlight. Sunlight reflected from the Moon is what we call moonlight.

The Moon is a sphere. When light shines on a sphere, the sphere is half lit and half dark. It doesn't matter where you position the sphere. It is always half lit and half dark.

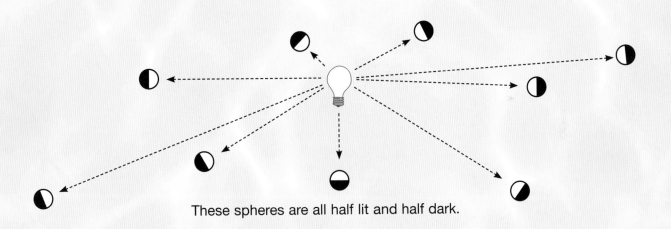

These spheres are all half lit and half dark.

The same is true for the Moon. It is always half sunlit and half dark. The half that is sunlit is the side toward the Sun. The half that is dark is the side away from the Sun.

The Moon's Position

The Moon never looks the same 2 days in a row. Its appearance changes all the time. Sometimes it is a thin sliver, and sometimes it is completely round. Why does the Moon's appearance change?

The Sun is in the center of the **solar system.** The planets orbit the Sun. And the Moon orbits Earth.

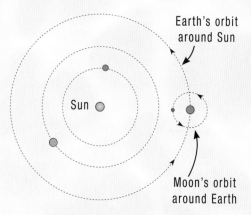

It takes 4 weeks for the Moon to go clear around Earth. The first thing to understand is where the Moon is during those 4 weeks. Let's take a look from out in space.

We'll start the observations when the Moon is at position 1 between Earth and the Sun.

The Moon orbits Earth in a counterclockwise direction. After 1 week the Moon has moved to position 2.

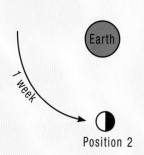

After 2 weeks the Moon has moved to position 3 on the other side of Earth. The Moon has traveled halfway around Earth.

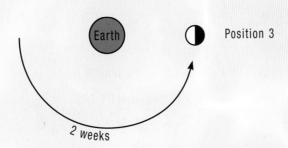

After 3 weeks the Moon has moved to position 4. It is now three-quarters of the way around Earth.

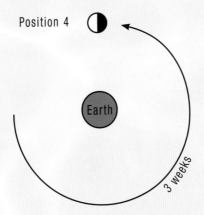

In another week (a total of 4 weeks) the Moon has returned to position 1. It has completed one **lunar cycle.**

Look at the Moon in each of the illustrations. You will see that the sunlit side is always toward the Sun. It doesn't matter where the Moon is in relation to Earth. The Moon's bright side is always toward the Sun.

The Moon's Appearance

The shape of the Moon doesn't change. It is always a sphere. The amount of the Moon that is brightly lit doesn't change. Half of the Moon is always sunlit. What changes is how much of the sunlit half is visible from Earth. You might see just a tiny bit of the sunlit half. Or you might see all of the sunlit half. The shape of the visible part of the Moon is called a **phase.**

Let's look at the phase of the Moon in position 1. The Moon is between the Sun and Earth. When you look up at the Moon from Earth, what do you see? Nothing. All of the sunlit half of the Moon is on the other side. This is the **new Moon.** The new Moon has no light showing. The new Moon is shown as a black circle.

Position 1

New Moon
This is what you see.

Let's move forward 2 weeks. The Moon has continued in its orbit and is now in position 3. Now what do you see when you look up at the Moon? The whole sunlit side of the Moon! This is the **full Moon.** The full Moon is shown as a white circle.

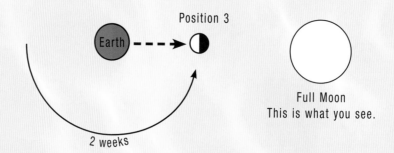

Position 3

2 weeks

Full Moon
This is what you see.

Now let's look at positions 2 and 4. At both positions you see half of the sunlit part of the Moon and half of the dark part of the Moon. At position 2, when you look up at the Moon, the sunlit part is on the right side. (Turn this book upside down to make sure.) At position 4 the sunlit part of the Moon is on the left. Position 2 is the **first-quarter Moon.** Position 4 is the **third-quarter Moon.**

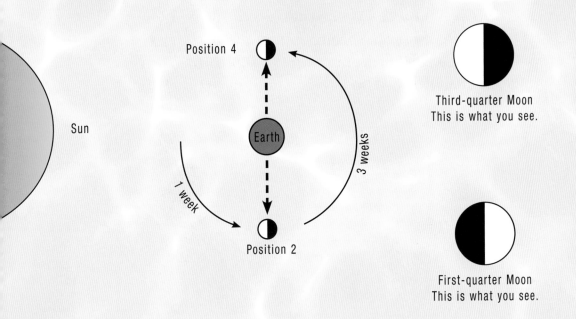

Third-quarter Moon
This is what you see.

First-quarter Moon
This is what you see.

The position of the Moon in its lunar cycle determines the Moon's phase.

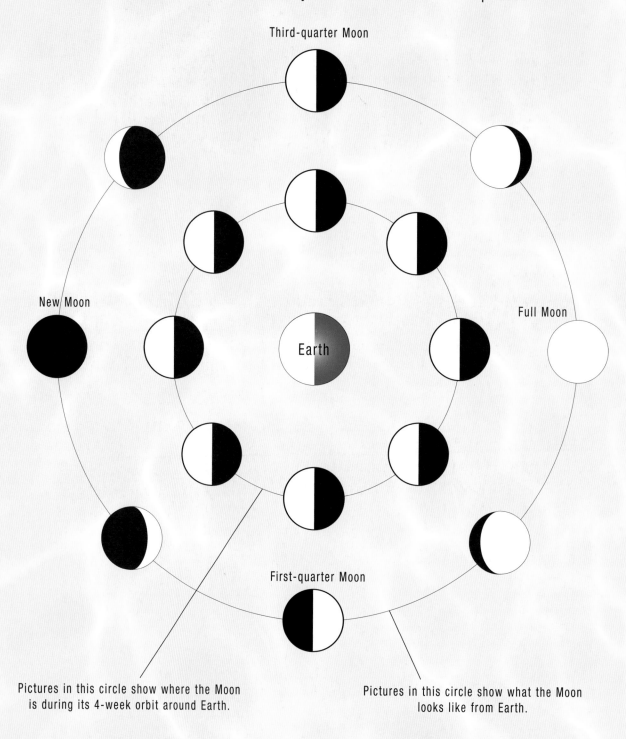

Pictures in this circle show where the Moon is during its 4-week orbit around Earth.

Pictures in this circle show what the Moon looks like from Earth.

The Lunar Cycle

The new Moon is invisible for two reasons. First, no light is coming to your eyes from the Moon. The sunlit side is on the farside. Second, to look for the new Moon, you would have to look right into the Sun. The glare is too bright to see the Moon.

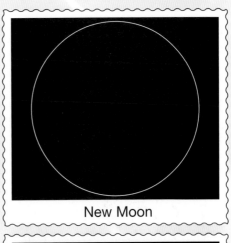
New Moon

Three days later the Moon has moved in its orbit and it is visible. The first sighting of the Moon after a new Moon is a tiny sliver of light. The curved shape is called the **crescent** Moon.

Day 3 waxing crescent Moon

On day 5 the Moon looks larger. About one-quarter of the Moon is now bright. Each day the bright part of the Moon is a little larger. We say the Moon is **waxing** when it appears to grow.

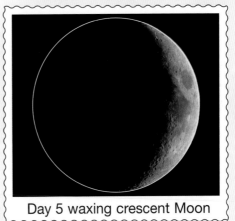
Day 5 waxing crescent Moon

By day 6 bright sunlight covers almost half the face of the Moon. This is the last day of the waxing crescent Moon. Tomorrow the Moon will appear as the first-quarter Moon.

Day 6 waxing crescent Moon

Day 7 first-quarter Moon

The first-quarter Moon is the phase seen on day 7. The Moon has completed the first quarter of its lunar cycle. Viewers on Earth see half the sunlit side of the Moon and half the dark side of the Moon. The brightly sunlit side is on the right side.

Day 9 waxing gibbous Moon

On day 9 you can see more than half the sunlit side of the Moon. The Moon appears to be oval shaped. A Moon phase that is larger than a quarter but not yet full is called a **gibbous** Moon. Because the day-10 Moon is still getting bigger, it is a waxing gibbous Moon.

Day 11 waxing gibbous Moon

On day 11 the Moon is almost round, but not quite. It is still a waxing gibbous Moon. Viewers on Earth can see most of the sunlit half of the Moon. They can see only a small sliver of the dark side of the Moon. Can you see the dark crescent?

Day 14 full Moon

On day 14 you can see the whole sunlit side of the Moon. This is full-Moon phase. A full Moon always rises at the same time the Sun sets.

Each day after the full Moon, the bright part of the Moon gets smaller. Getting smaller is called **waning.** On day 18 the Moon looks oval again. Because it is still between full-Moon phase and quarter phase, it is still a gibbous Moon, a waning gibbous Moon.

Day 18 waning gibbous Moon

On day 21 the Moon has completed three-quarters of its orbit around Earth. The Moon appears as the third quarter, again half bright and half dark. But notice that the bright side of the third-quarter phase is on the left. Compare the appearance of the third-quarter Moon and the first-quarter Moon.

Day 21 third-quarter Moon

As the Moon starts the last 7 days of its orbit, it returns to crescent phase. But because it is getting smaller each day, it is the waning crescent phase. By day 24, a viewer on Earth sees just a small part of the sunlit side of the Moon. A lot of the dark side is visible again.

Day 24 waning crescent Moon

On about day 28 the Moon has completed one lunar cycle. It is back at its starting point. It is new-Moon phase again. The night sky is moonless. The day sky has no Moon. For a couple of days viewers on Earth are out of touch with the Moon.

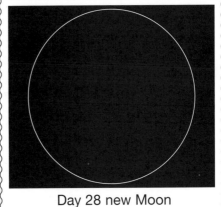
Day 28 new Moon

Then, in the evening sky, just after sunset, the Moon reappears. It is a thin, silver crescent. And if you are in the right place at the right time, you could see something special. It is a bright crescent on the edge of a dim full Moon. It is called the old Moon in the new Moon's arms.

Old Moon in the new Moon's arms

How can you see a bright crescent Moon and a pale full Moon at the same time? When the Moon appears as a thin crescent, it is almost between Earth and the Sun. A lot of light reflects from Earth onto the Moon. The whole Moon is dimly lit by earthshine.

Old Moon in the new Moon's arms

Review Questions

1. How long does it take Earth's Moon to complete one lunar cycle?

2. What is a new Moon and what causes it?

3. What is the difference between a waxing Moon and a waning Moon?

4. What is the difference between a crescent Moon and a gibbous Moon?

5. Describe the Moon's appearance 1 week, 2 weeks, 3 weeks, and 4 weeks after the new Moon.

Summary: The Moon

People used to think that everything they saw in the sky revolved around Earth. This included the Sun and the **stars.** We know now that Earth is a **planet** that **orbits** the Sun. It is one of eight planets in the solar system. The **Moon** orbits Earth. It takes about 4 weeks for the Moon to orbit Earth.

Sometimes you can see the Moon at night. Sometimes you can see it during the day. That's because the Moon orbits Earth once every 4 weeks.

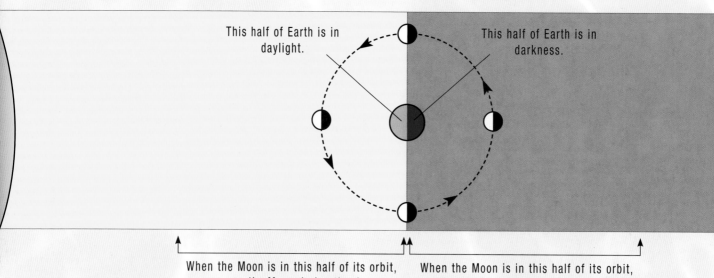

This half of Earth is in daylight.

This half of Earth is in darkness.

When the Moon is in this half of its orbit, we see the Moon during the day.

When the Moon is in this half of its orbit, we see the Moon during the night.

The Moon doesn't always appear to be the same shape. That's because half of the Moon is always dark. The other half is sunlit. As the Moon orbits Earth, observers on Earth see different amounts of the sunlit half. The different shapes of the Moon are called **phases.** The phases change in a regular pattern as the Moon orbits Earth. The Moon completes an orbit and a **lunar cycle** every 4 weeks.

There are four specific phases that happen about 1 week apart. The **new Moon** is invisible. It occurs when the Moon is between Earth and the Sun. The **full Moon** occurs when Earth is between the Sun and the Moon. Halfway between the new Moon and the full Moon is the **first-quarter Moon.** Halfway between the full Moon and the new Moon is the **third-quarter Moon.**

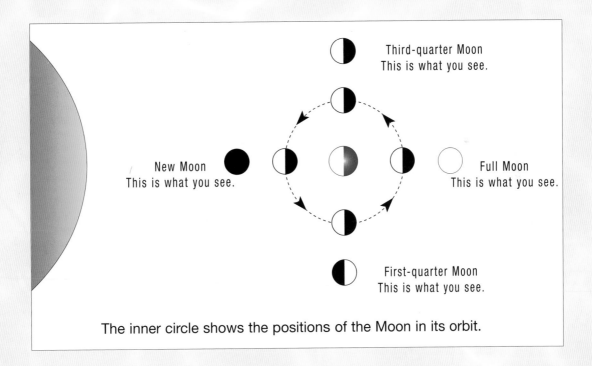

Third-quarter Moon
This is what you see.

New Moon
This is what you see.

Full Moon
This is what you see.

First-quarter Moon
This is what you see.

The inner circle shows the positions of the Moon in its orbit.

31

The Moon changes through its phases in a predictable pattern. The first appearance of the Moon after the new Moon is a thin **crescent.** The next day the crescent will be a little bigger. And the crescent will get bigger each day until the first-quarter Moon. Getting bigger is called **waxing.** After the first quarter the Moon continues waxing. But it is no longer a crescent Moon. It is a **gibbous** Moon. Gibbous Moons are oval shaped. The gibbous Moon waxes until it is completely round. That is the full Moon.

For the next 2 weeks the Moon is **waning.** Each day it is a little smaller. The waning gibbous Moon becomes the third-quarter Moon. Then the Moon becomes a waning crescent Moon. At the end of 4 weeks the lunar cycle is complete, and the Moon is new again.

Say you drew the appearance of the Moon for a month. If you put the drawings in order, this is what you would see. This is the lunar cycle you will observe month after month.

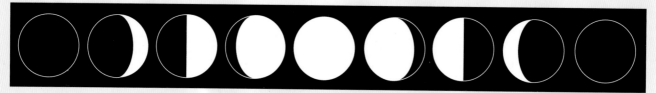

Lunar month drawings

Lunar month photos

Summary Questions

Now is a good time to review what you have recorded in your science notebook. Think about Earth's place in the solar system and how the Moon's appearance changes during the 4-week lunar cycle.

1. How do the Sun, Earth, and the Moon move around in the solar system?

2. Why does it appear that the Moon changes shape?

3. Starting with the new Moon, how do the phases change over 4 weeks?

Vocabulary

star

planet

orbit

Moon

phase

lunar cycle

new Moon

full Moon

first-quarter Moon

third-quarter Moon

crescent

waxing

gibbous

waning

Extensions

Math Problem of the Week

In a make-believe planetary system, three planets orbit a star. The closest planet is Alfar, and the middle planet is Baytar. The planet farthest from the star is Gammar.

Planet Gammar orbits the star in 360 days. So the Gammar year is 360 days long. Baytar orbits in 240 days. Alfar orbits in 120 days.

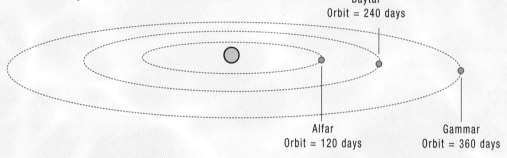

One day all three planets were lined up.

1. How many Gammar years will it be until the three planets line up again?

2. How many orbits will Gammar make before they line up again?

3. How many orbits will Alfar and Baytar make?

Home/School Connection

Over the years each full Moon picked up folk names that had special meaning. Some are obvious, like the Harvest Moon of September. Others are more mysterious. Try to figure out why each full Moon got that name.

Make up your own list of names for the full Moons. Bring your list to school to share.

Month	Full Moon Folk Name
January	Moon after Yule, Old Moon
February	Snow Moon, Hunger Moon, Wolf Moon
March	Sap Moon, Crow Moon
April	Grass Moon, Egg Moon
May	Planting Moon, Milk Moon
June	Rose Moon, Strawberry Moon
July	Thunder Moon, Hay Moon
August	Green Corn Moon, Grain Moon
September	Fruit Moon, Harvest Moon
October	Hunter's Moon
November	Frosty Moon, Beaver Moon
December	Moon before Yule, Long Night Moon

Stargazing

Stars are twinkling points of light in the night sky. When you tuck into bed at night, the sky is filled with them. But in the morning they are gone. Where did they go?

The stars didn't go anywhere. They are exactly where they were when you went to sleep. But you can't see the stars in the daytime sky. This is because the light from our star, the Sun, is so bright.

Where Are the Stars?

Stars are huge balls of hot gas. Most stars are located in groups of stars called **galaxies.** The Sun is in the galaxy called the **Milky Way.** There are several hundred billion other stars in the Milky Way with us. If we could see the Milky Way, it might look something like the picture below. Our Sun is out on one of the arms where the arrow is pointing.

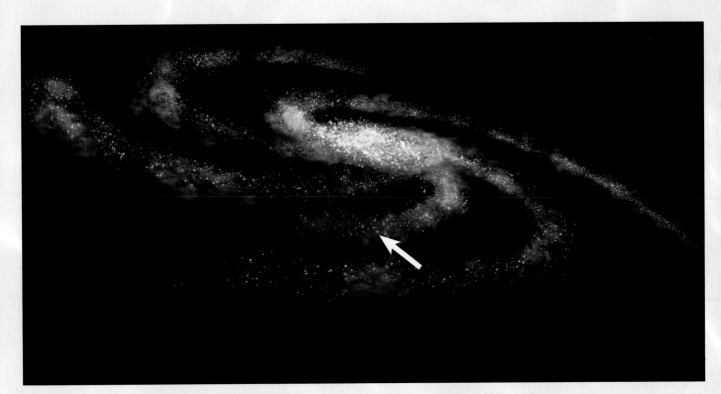

The Sun is one of the billions of stars in the Milky Way galaxy.

As you can see, we are surrounded by stars. Think about all the thousands of stars you can see and the billions of stars you can't see. All these stars are in the Milky Way galaxy. And all the stars, including the Sun, are moving slowly around in a huge circle. Because all the stars move together, the positions of the stars never change. You can see the same stars in the same places in the sky year after year.

Did you ever see the **Big Dipper?** It is seven bright stars in the shape of a dipper. The Big Dipper is part of a **constellation** called Ursa Major, or the Great Bear.

Most of the stars you see in the night sky are part of a constellation. A constellation is a group of stars in a pattern. Thousands of years ago stargazers imagined they could see animals and people in the star groups. And they gave names to the groups. Some of them are Orion the hunter, Scorpius the scorpion, Aquila the eagle, Leo the lion, and Gemini the twins. Those same exact constellations are still seen in the sky today. They are unchanged.

Constellations in Motion

Even though the stars don't change position, they appear to move across the night sky. Stars move across the sky for the same reason that the Sun and Moon move across the sky. The stars are not moving. Earth is moving. As Earth **rotates** on its **axis,** constellations rise in the east. They travel across the night sky and set in the west.

If you look at the stars every day for a year, you will see something interesting. The stars you see in the winter are different than the stars you see in the summer. If the stars don't move around, how is that possible? To see why, we have to look at how Earth orbits the Sun.

Here is a simple drawing of the Milky Way galaxy. The Sun and Earth appear much larger than they really are. That's so we can study what happens as the seasons go by.

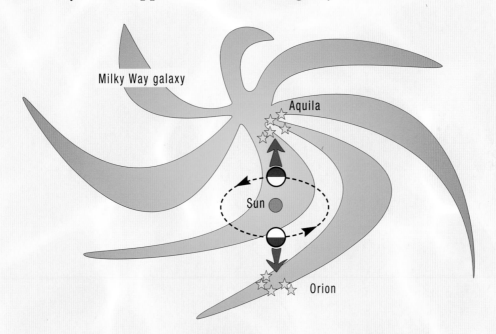

A simple drawing of the Sun ● and Earth ◒, not drawn to scale

The side of Earth facing the Sun is always in daylight. The side facing away from the Sun is always in darkness. You can only see stars when you are on the dark half of Earth.

When it is summer in California, Earth is between the Sun and the center of the Milky Way galaxy. The constellation Aquila is in that direction. The dark side of Earth is toward the center of the galaxy in the summer. On a summer night you see Aquila high overhead.

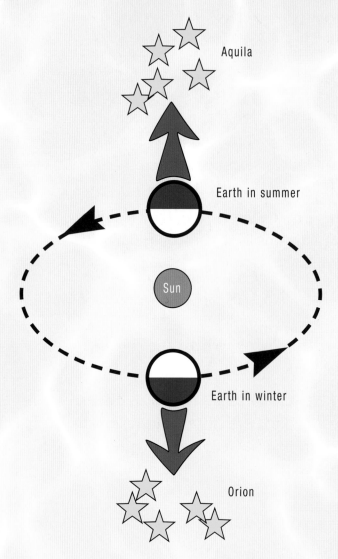

A simple drawing of the Sun and Earth, not drawn to scale

Six months later, Earth is on the other side of the Sun. It is winter in California. Now the dark side of Earth faces away from the center of the galaxy. The constellation Orion is in that direction. On a winter night you see Orion high overhead.

This is Orion. Can you see his belt and sword? The most important stars in the Orion constellation are in this pattern.

The constellation Orion is visible in the winter sky.

You should be able to see those stars in this photograph. And you should be able to see Orion in the sky on a clear winter night.

Think about this when you see Orion. You are seeing the same pattern of stars that a hundred generations of stargazers looked at before you. And a hundred generations into the future, stargazers will still see Orion marching across the winter sky.

Review Questions

1. **Why do stars move across the night sky?**

2. **What is a constellation?**

3. **Why are the constellations seen in the summer sky different than those seen in the winter sky?**

4. **Imagine that you could see stars during the daytime. What constellation would you see at noon in the winter? Why do you think so?**

Looking through Telescopes

What do you see when you look at the sky on a clear night? You probably see a lot of twinkling stars. Maybe you see the Moon or a planet. People saw the same objects in the sky thousands of years ago.

The way we look at objects in the sky changed in 1608. In that year the **telescope** was invented. A telescope is a tool that **magnifies** distant objects so they appear larger and closer.

Galileo Galilei

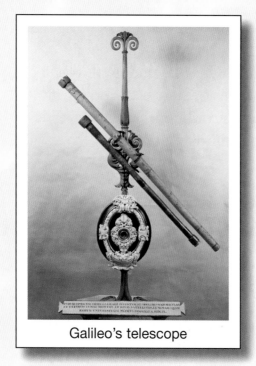
Galileo's telescope

Galileo Galilei (1564–1642) was a scientist who lived in Italy. In 1609 he was the first person to use a telescope to look at the night sky. He could see many more stars through the telescope than with his unaided eyes. He could see mountains and craters on the Moon. And he could see that planets were spheres, not just points of light. Then Galileo turned his telescope toward Jupiter. He became the first person to see moons orbiting another planet.

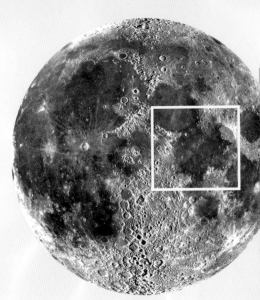

The *Apollo 11* landing site on the Moon

As telescopes got more powerful, **astronomers** could see more details on planets. They could also see more stars in the night sky. By the mid-1900s, the surface of the Moon could be studied in detail with telescopes on Earth. Scientists used pictures taken through telescopes to plan the first Moon landing in 1969.

Modern Telescopes

Most telescopes are found on mountain peaks. That puts them above most of the dust and pollution in the air. And they are far away from city lights. The telescopes are protected inside dome-shaped buildings called **observatories.**

Keck Observatory is on top of Mauna Kea, a 4,206-meter peak on the Big Island of Hawaii.

Hubble Space Telescope was put into orbit around Earth in 1990.

The space shuttle placed a very special telescope in Earth's orbit in 1990. It is called the Hubble Space Telescope. The Hubble telescope takes pictures of planets and other objects in the solar system. And it takes pictures of objects beyond the solar system. Because the telescope is located above Earth's atmosphere, it gets a clear view of outer space.

Mars seen from Hubble Space Telescope

When you look up at the sky on a clear, moonless night, you can see about 2,000 stars. But that view changes a lot when you look through the Hubble Space Telescope. You can see millions of stars that are too dim to see with your unaided eyes. Telescopes make distant objects look bigger and closer. With telescopes, astronomers can explore space without leaving Earth.

The Milky Way seen with the unaided eye on a clear night.

Part of the Milky Way seen through the Hubble Space Telescope.

Review Questions

1. **Who was Galileo and what was he the first to do?**

2. **Why is a telescope a useful tool to an astronomer?**

3. **Why are modern telescopes built on mountaintops or put into space?**

Star Scientists

Sometimes a childhood fascination with stars lasts a lifetime. Scientists who try to find out the secrets of stars are called astronomers. Meet three scientists who have taken star study in different directions. They truly are star scientists.

Black Holes

Stephen Hawking

When you drop a ball on Earth, the force of **gravity** pulls it down. Gravity keeps your feet on the ground, too. When a star reaches the end of its life, it collapses. All the **matter** in the star is pulled together because of gravity. In collapsed stars, gravity can even pull in light.

When a really big star collapses, it can become a **black hole.** In a black hole, gravity is so strong that nothing, not even light, can escape. Everything for millions of kilometers around is pulled into the black hole, where it disappears.

Today the best-known scientist who studies black holes is Stephen Hawking (1942–). Hawking was born 300 years after the death of Galileo. Using mathematics, Hawking helped prove that black holes exist.

Since 1994, the Hubble Space Telescope has been used to search for evidence of black holes. Hubble images show stars and gases swirling toward a central point. Hawking says this could be the effect of a black hole. A black hole's strong gravity would pull in everything around it, including stars. Future images from Hubble might help scientists improve their understanding of black holes.

Is There Life on Other Planets?

Lots of people wonder if there is life anyplace else in the universe. But Edna DeVore (1947–) does more than wonder. She works at the SETI Institute. SETI is short for Search for Extraterrestrial Intelligence.

The scientists at SETI think that there may be other intelligent beings in the universe. If they are out there, they will live on a planet orbiting a star. And intelligent life will develop technologies that send signals out into space. Radio, TV, navigation systems, and telephones on Earth send messages in all directions into space. Is someone else out there doing the same thing?

Edna DeVore

The SETI Institute watches the stars for any signs of life in the universe. They use big sets of antennas to listen for any sounds of life, like radio signals.

DeVore is a scientist and educator at SETI. She grew up on a ranch in Sattley, California. DeVore remembers watching the stars and the Milky Way in the clear night sky as a child. But the thought of being a star scientist didn't cross her mind at that time. It was when she was in college that DeVore became more and more interested in the stars. After getting her degree in astronomy, she was a teacher and a planetarium director. But the question she always asked herself was, "Are we alone in the universe?"

DeVore is now in charge of education and public information for the SETI Institute. And what's the latest report from the universe? The scientists at SETI haven't heard or seen anything yet. But they still keep watching and listening.

What Is a Planetarium?

You put water and fish in an aquarium. You put soil and plants in a terrarium. But what do you put in a planetarium? Planets! A **planetarium** is filled with planets, stars, galaxies, and everything else seen in the night sky.

Neil deGrasse Tyson

A planetarium is a theater with a dome-shaped ceiling. In the middle of the room is a projector. The projector shines points of light all over the dome. The points of light are in the same positions as the stars in the sky. The projected stars make it seem as though you are outside watching the stars.

One of the fun things about a planetarium is that you can control the night sky. Want to see the stars as they were the day you were born? Or how the sky looked at different times in Earth's history? The projector operator can put you under the stars at any time and any place.

When he was a child, Neil deGrasse Tyson (1959–) never dreamed that he would one day be in charge of a planetarium. Tyson took a class at the Hayden Planetarium in New York City when he was in middle school. He was awarded a certificate at the end of the class. It meant a lot to him.

Tyson's love of the stars grew as he got older. After getting a PhD in astrophysics, Tyson spent time doing research and promoting education. He researched how stars form and explained space science to the public. He works hard to make science interesting for everyone. In 1996 Tyson became the youngest person ever to direct the Hayden Planetarium. It is the same place he visited as a child.

Summary: The Stars

Stars are huge balls of hot gas. They produce bright light that streams out into space. When we go outdoors on a clear night, we see the stars as tiny points of light. There are billions of them sending light our way. But because most of them are so far away, the light is too dim for us to see. We can enjoy the 2,000 or so that we can see with our unaided eyes.

Astronomers study stars and other objects in the sky. One of the most important tools they use is the **telescope.** Telescopes **magnify** objects in the sky. When an astronomer looks at an object through a telescope, the object looks bigger and closer. With a telescope, many more stars can be seen. Objects in the night sky can be studied in greater detail with a telescope.

The first person to use a telescope to look at the Moon and planets was the great Italian scientist Galileo. He saw things no one had ever seen before. He saw mountains and craters on the Moon and moons orbiting the planet Jupiter. Galileo's telescope brought the science of astronomy to a new level.

Galileo's painting of the surface of Earth's Moon

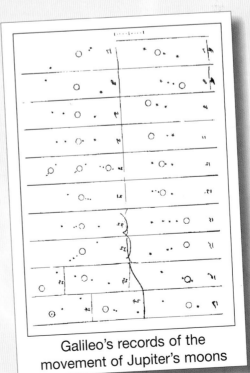

Galileo's records of the movement of Jupiter's moons

Moving Objects in the Sky

The Sun, the Moon, and the stars all move in the sky. But they all move in a different way. The Sun is easy. It rises in the east in the morning and sets in the west at night. The Sun is seen only during the day, never at night. Every day it does the same thing.

The Moon is a little harder to figure out. It rises in the east and sets in the west, just like the Sun. But it doesn't always rise and set at the same time. Sometimes it rises in the morning, and sometimes it rises in the afternoon. And the Moon is seen during the day and the night.

The Moon and Sun rise in the east and set in the west because Earth **rotates** on its axis. To people on Earth it looks like the Sun and Moon are moving across the sky. The Moon rises and sets at different times because the Moon is orbiting Earth. The Moon is changing its position all the time.

Stars are different. They are seen only at night. They are up in the sky all the time. But we can't see them during the day because the Sun is too bright. As soon as the Sun sets, it gets dark. Then we can see the stars. Stars rise and set, too. If you watch one star, you can see it rise above the eastern horizon. It then moves across the night sky, and sets in the west. Why? Because Earth is rotating.

Earth's Orbit

One more thing is different about stars. Earth is completely surrounded by stars in all directions. But you can't see all of them at once. This is because half of them are on the day side of Earth. And the stars you can see in the winter are different than the ones you can see in the summer.

Here's why. Earth orbits the Sun. One complete orbit takes a year. At all times, half of Earth is in daylight and half is in darkness. It is always the side of Earth toward the Sun that is in daylight. The day side of Earth is always "looking" toward the Sun.

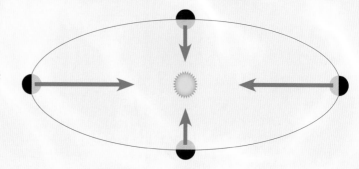

48

The side of Earth away from the Sun is always in darkness. The dark side of Earth is "looking" away from the Sun all year long. We can see stars only at night when it is dark. So stargazers always look in the opposite direction from the Sun.

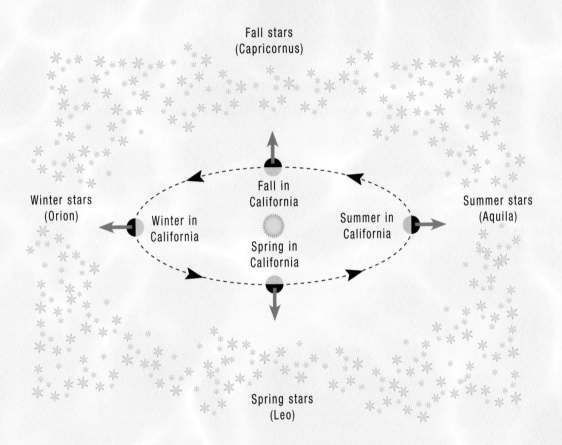

As Earth orbits the Sun, the dark side of Earth is aimed at different parts of the star-filled sky. Because stars don't move, the stars and **constellations** you see change from season to season.

In California, look for Aquila the eagle in summer. Look for Capricornus the goat in the fall, Orion the hunter in winter, and Leo the lion in spring.

Summary Questions

Now is a good time to review what you have recorded in your science notebook. Think about the stars and constellations in the night sky and how they seem to move in the sky during the night and from season to season.

1. What makes telescopes useful to astronomers?

2. What is a constellation?

3. Why do we see different stars in the summer and winter night skies?

Vocabulary

astronomer

telescope

magnify

rotate

constellation

Extensions

Math Problem of the Week

Tito has a telescope. He has five different eyepiece lenses. Each one is a different strength. They are 2x, 4x, 10x, 20x, and a mystery eyepiece that was unmarked. The x means "times." So a 100x eyepiece makes an object look 100 times larger.

Tito put the 2x eyepiece on his telescope. He pointed his telescope toward the Moon. The Moon looked 4 centimeters across. Tito tried the 10x eyepiece, and the Moon looked 20 centimeters across.

1. How big did the Moon look when Tito used the 4x and 20x eyepieces?

2. The Moon looked 30 centimeters across when Tito used the mystery eyepiece. What is the strength of the mystery eyepiece?

3. Tito wants to see the Moon 50 centimeters across. What strength eyepiece should he get?

References

Learning More about Sun, Moon, and Stars

Investigate Eclipses

What is an eclipse of the Sun? What is a lunar eclipse? Find out what causes eclipses. Set up a demonstration that shows eclipses of the Sun and Moon.

Find Out about the Apollo Program

Find out about the NASA Apollo missions. What did they do? These websites are good places to start.

Earth's Moon: Kid's Eye View

http://solarsystem.nasa.gov/planets/profile.cfm?Object=Moon&Display=Kids

The Apollo Program (Smithsonian National Air and Space Museum)

www.nasm.si.edu/collections/imagery/apollo/apollo.htm

Read Moon Myths and Legends

Prescientific cultures told stories about the origin of the Moon, phases of the Moon, and constellations. The stories also told of other things people observed in the night sky. Search for myths and legends in the library or on the Internet. Share these stories with your class.

Use Star Maps

Star maps show the locations of stars and constellations in the night sky. FOSSweb has seasonal star maps you can view and download. Go to www.FOSSweb.com. Click Grades 3–6, then Sun, Moon, and Stars. The Star Maps are in the Activities box.

Choose the star map for the month you will be looking at stars. Take the map outside on a clear night. How many constellations can you identify?

FOSSweb

Go to www.FOSSweb.com to find activities for each FOSS module. You will also find interesting books to read, vocabulary lists, and links to related websites. This site was designed for you to use with friends and family at home. For your parents, there is information about each FOSS module and copies of the Home/School Connections.

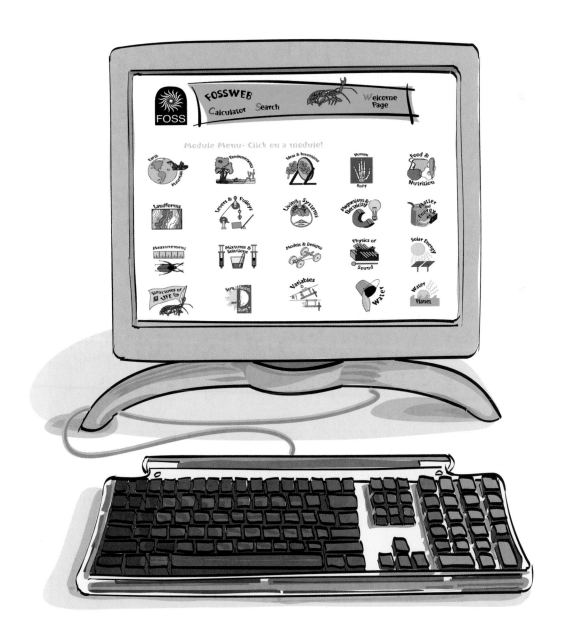

Science Safety Rules

1. Listen carefully to your teacher's instructions. Follow all directions. Ask questions if you don't know what to do.

2. Tell your teacher if you have any allergies.

3. Never put any materials in your mouth. Do not taste anything unless your teacher tells you to do so.

4. Never smell any unknown material. If your teacher tells you to smell something, wave your hand over the material to bring the smell toward your nose.

5. Do not touch your face, mouth, ears, eyes, or nose while working with chemicals, plants, or animals.

6. Always protect your eyes. Wear safety goggles when necessary. Tell your teacher if you wear contact lenses. Never look directly at the Sun.

7. Always wash your hands with soap and warm water after handling chemicals, plants, or animals.

8. Never mix any chemicals unless your teacher tells you to do so.

9. Report all spills, accidents, and injuries to your teacher.

10. Treat animals with respect, caution, and consideration.

11. Clean up your work space after each investigation.

12. Act responsibly during all science activities.

Glossary

Astronomer   A scientist who studies objects in the universe including the stars, planets, and moons.

Axis   An imaginary line around which a sphere, like a planet, rotates.

Big Dipper   A group of seven bright stars in the shape of a dipper.

Black hole   A region in space without light that has a strong gravitational pull. A black hole is caused by the collapse of stars.

Constellation   A group of stars humans observe in a pattern and give a name.

Crescent   A word used to describe the curved shape of the visible part of the Moon before and after a new Moon.

Cycle   A set of events or actions that repeat in a predictable pattern.

Day   The time between sunrise and sunset on Earth when it is light.

First-quarter Moon   A phase of the Moon in the lunar cycle halfway between a new Moon and a full Moon. The Moon appears to be a "half Moon" as seen from Earth.

Full Moon   A phase of the Moon in the lunar cycle when all of the sunlit side of the Moon is visible from Earth.

Galaxy   A group of billions of stars. Earth is in the Milky Way galaxy.

Gibbous   A word used to describe the Moon when it appears to be more than half but less than full.

Gravity   A force that pulls objects toward each other.

Horizon   The apparent boundary between Earth's surface and the sky.

Lunar cycle   The 4-week period during which the Moon orbits Earth one time and goes through all of its phases.

Magnify   To make an object appear larger in size.

Matter   Anything that takes up space and has mass.

Milky Way   One of the billions of galaxies that make up the universe. The Sun is one of the billions of stars in the Milky Way galaxy.

Moon   Earth's natural satellite.

New Moon   The phase of the Moon in the lunar cycle when the sunlit side of the Moon is not visible from Earth.

Night   The time between sunset and sunrise on Earth when it is dark.

Observatory   A building that protects telescopes. Observatories are often found on mountain peaks above the dust and pollution in the air.

Orbit   To move or travel around an object in a curved path. Earth orbits the Sun. The Moon orbits Earth.

Phase   The shape of the visible part of the Moon.

Planet   A large, celestial body orbiting a star.

Planetarium   A theater with a dome-shaped ceiling that represents the sky. Planets, stars, and galaxies can be projected on the inside of the dome.

Predictable   To estimate accurately in advance based on a pattern or previous knowledge.

Reflect   To bounce off an object or surface. Light reflects from the Moon.

Rotate   To turn on an axis.

Satellite   An object, such as a moon, that orbits another object, such as a planet.

Season   The four times during the year that bring predictable weather conditions to a region on Earth. The four seasons are spring, summer, fall, and winter.

Shadow   The dark area behind an object that blocks light.

Solar system   The Sun and the planets and other objects that orbit the Sun.

Star   A huge sphere of hydrogen and helium that radiates heat and light. The Sun is a star.

Sun   The star around which Earth and other planets orbit.

Sunlight   Light from the Sun.

Sunrise   The time of day when the Sun is coming over the horizon in the east.

Sunset   The time of day when the Sun is going below the horizon in the west.

Telescope   An optical instrument that makes objects appear closer and larger.

Third-quarter Moon   The phase of the Moon in the lunar cycle halfway between the full Moon and the new Moon. The Moon appears from Earth to be a "half Moon."

Unaided eyes   Looking at something without the use of a telescope or microscope.

Waning   Getting smaller.

Waxing   Getting larger.

Index

Photo Credits

About the Cover: An astronomer views Venus and the crescent Moon in a twilight sky from the Grand Canyon's South Rim in Grand Canyon National Park, Arizona.